One thing you can say about living alone . . .

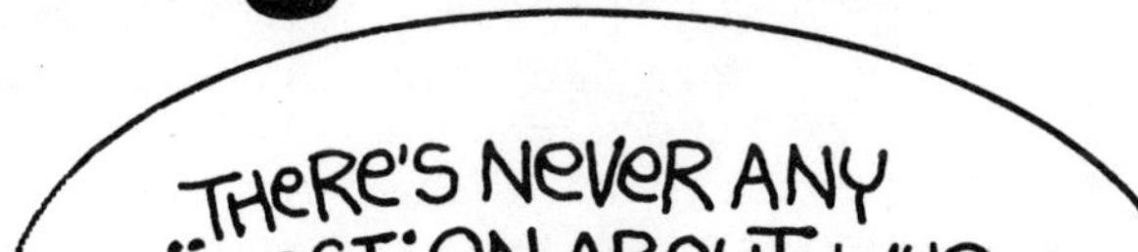
...THERE'S NEVER ANY QUESTION ABOUT WHO DIDN'T JIGGLE THE HANDLE ON THE JOHN !!

Andrews and McMeel, Inc.
A Universal Press Syndicate Company
Kansas City • New York • Washington

ZIGGY™ is syndicated internationally by Universal Press Syndicate

 For information write Andrews and McMeel, Inc., a Universal Press Syndicate Company, 4400 Johnson Drive, Fairway, Kansas 66205.

ISBN: 0-8362-1967-8
Library of Congress Catalog Card Number: 81-65623

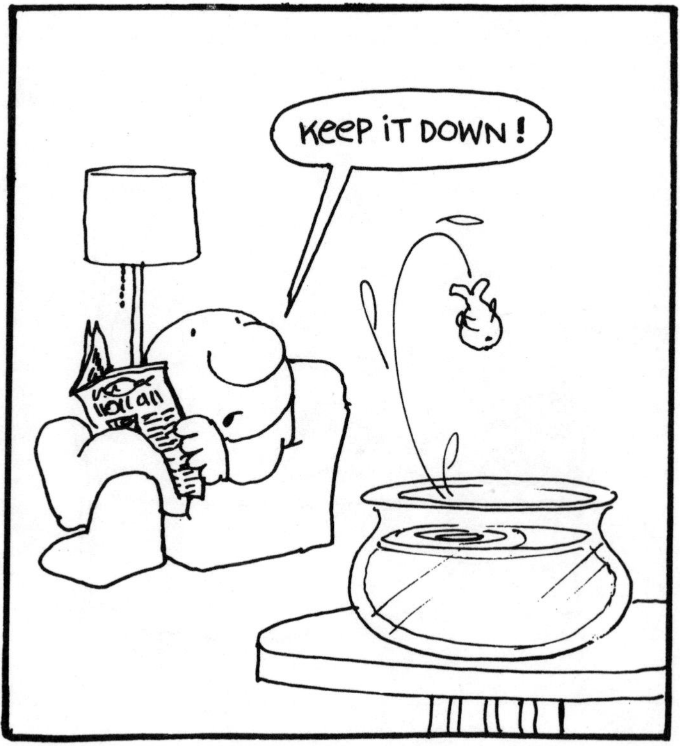
KEEP IT DOWN!

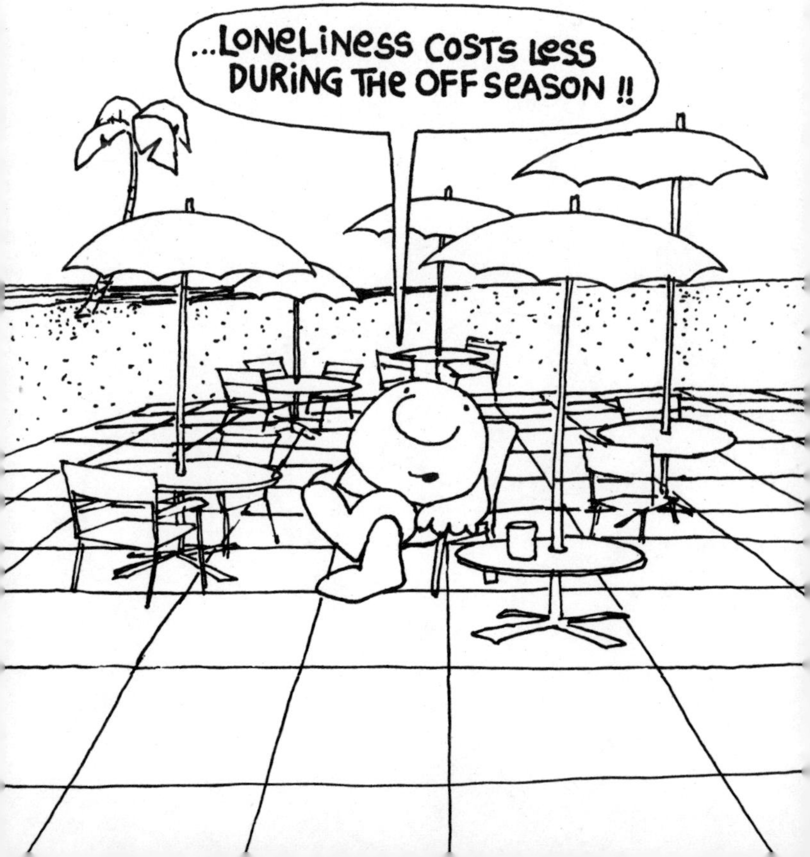
...LONELINESS COSTS LESS DURING THE OFF SEASON !!

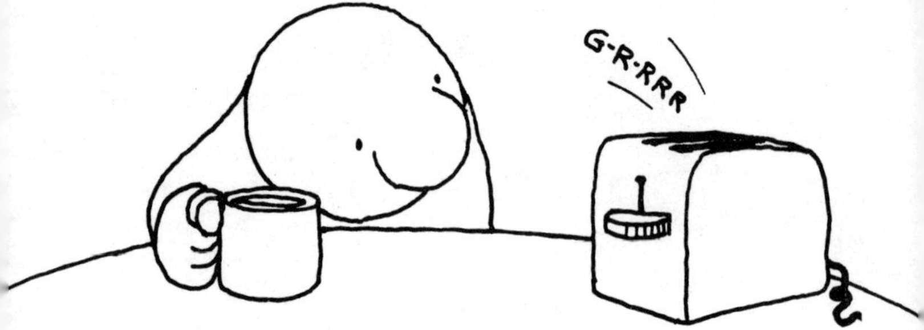
G-R-RRR

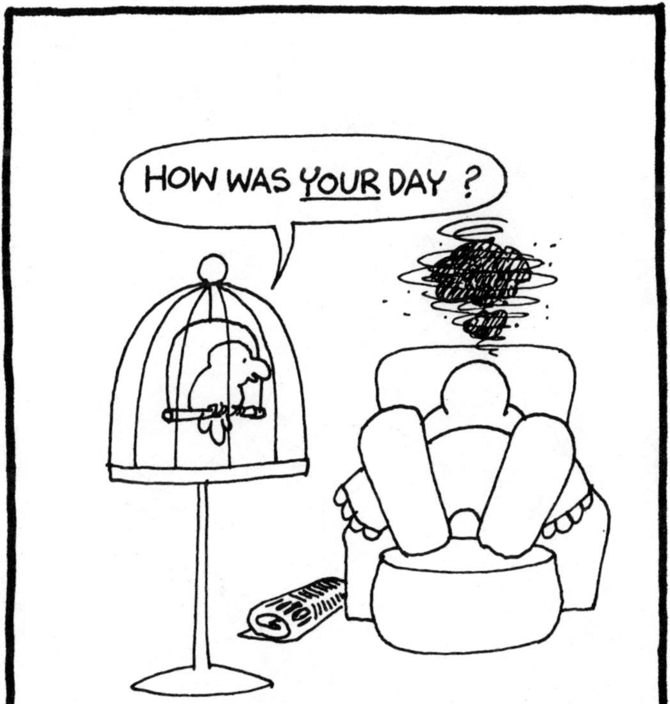
HOW WAS YOUR DAY ?

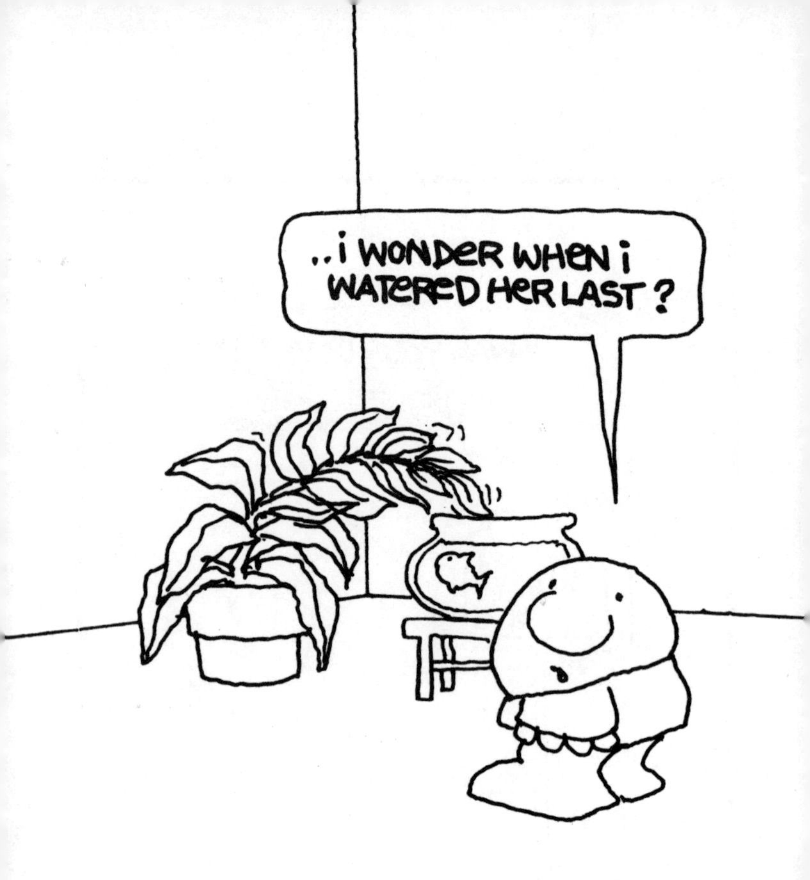
..i WONDER WHEN i WATERED HER LAST ?

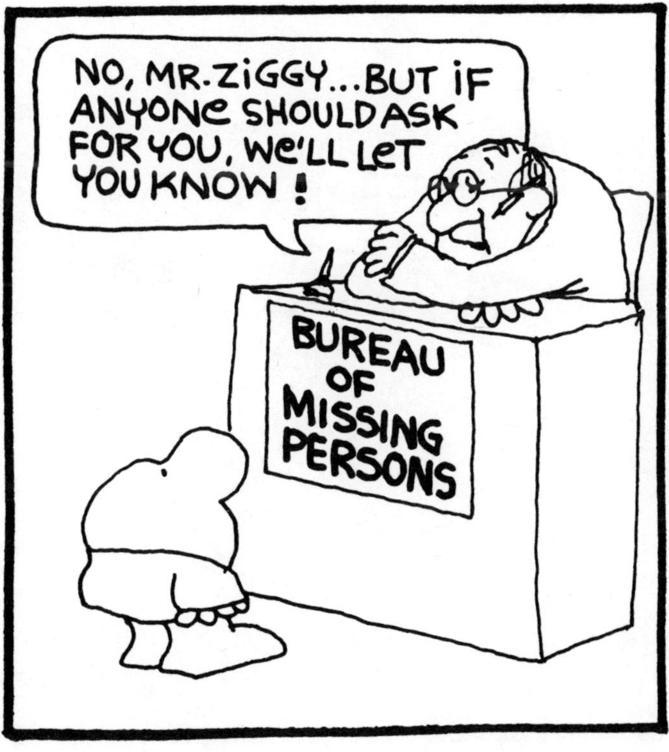
NO, MR. ZIGGY... BUT IF ANYONE SHOULD ASK FOR YOU, WE'LL LET YOU KNOW!
BUREAU OF MISSING PERSONS

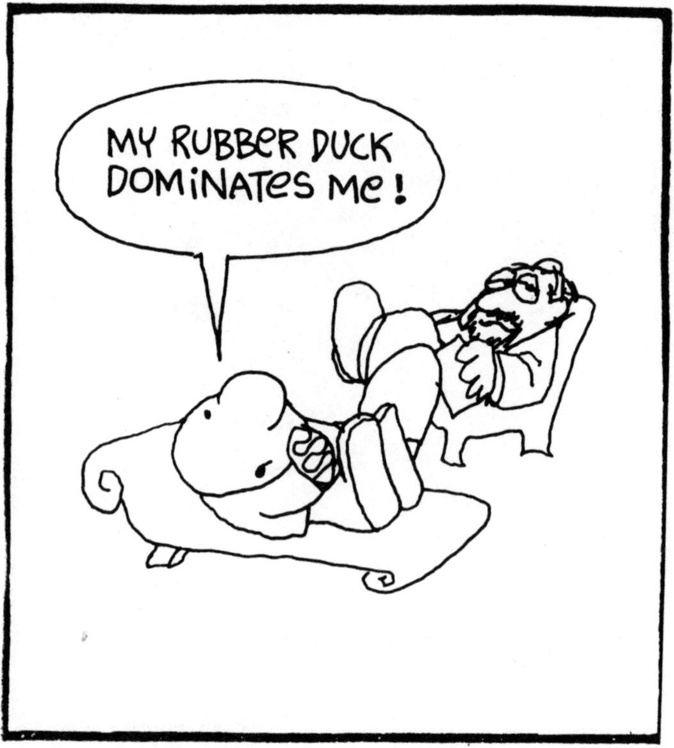
MY RUBBER DUCK DOMINATES ME!

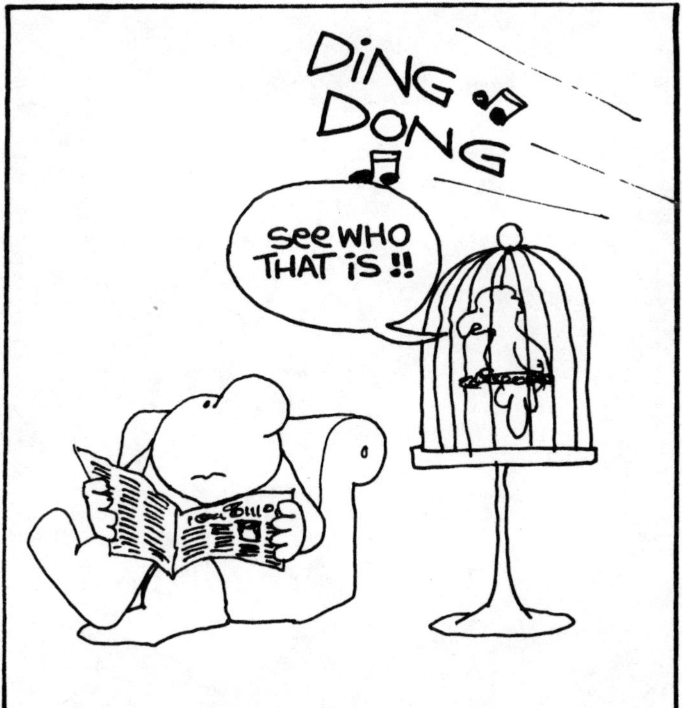
DING DONG
SEE WHO THAT IS !!

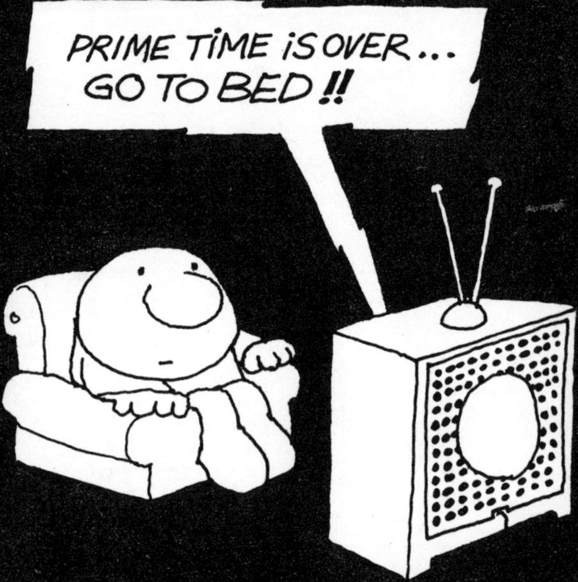
PRIME TIME IS OVER...
GO TO BED!!

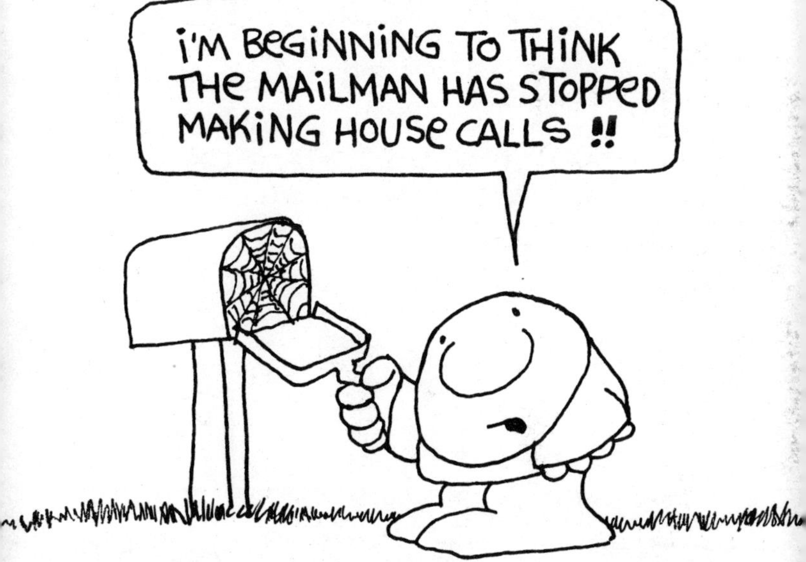
I'M BEGINNING TO THINK THE MAILMAN HAS STOPPED MAKING HOUSE CALLS !!

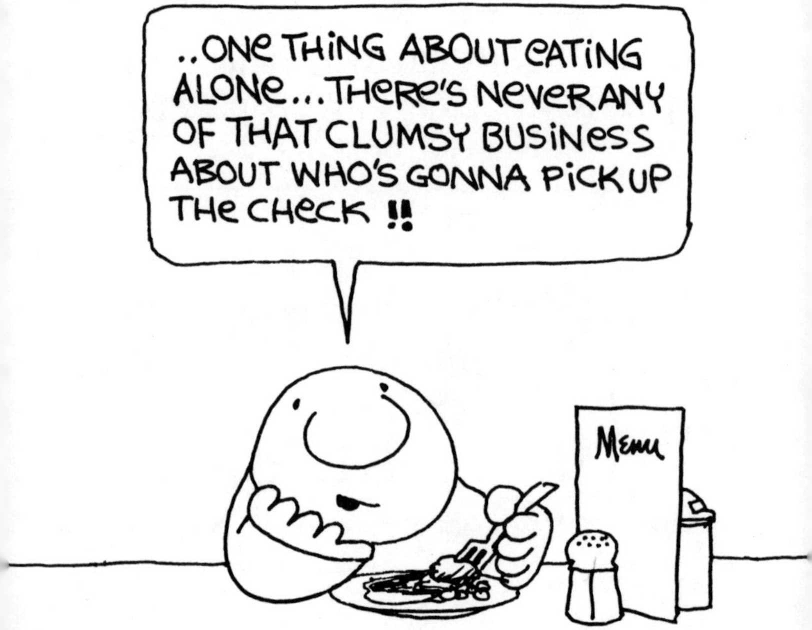
..ONE THING ABOUT EATING ALONE...THERE'S NEVER ANY OF THAT CLUMSY BUSINESS ABOUT WHO'S GONNA PICK UP THE CHECK !!
MENU

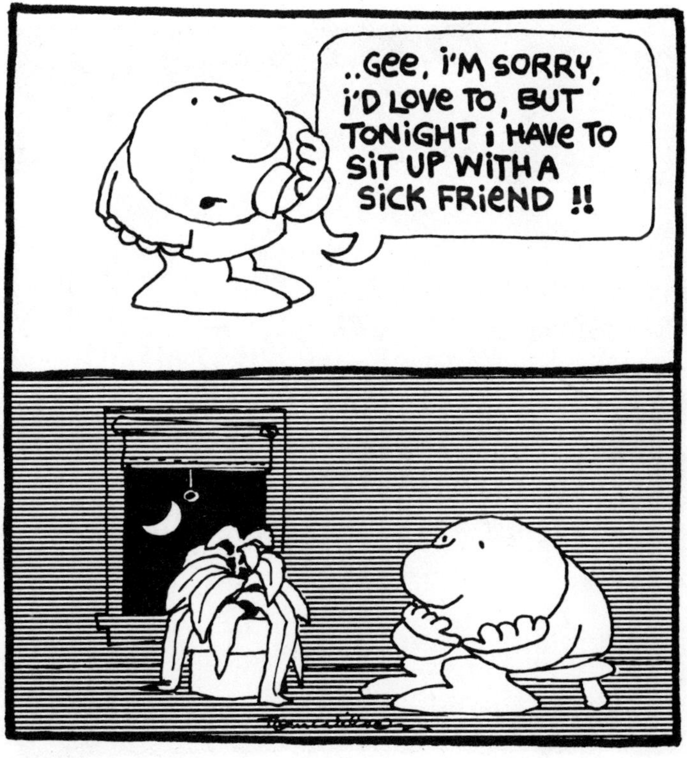
..GEE, I'M SORRY, I'D LOVE TO, BUT TONIGHT I HAVE TO SIT UP WITH A SICK FRIEND !!

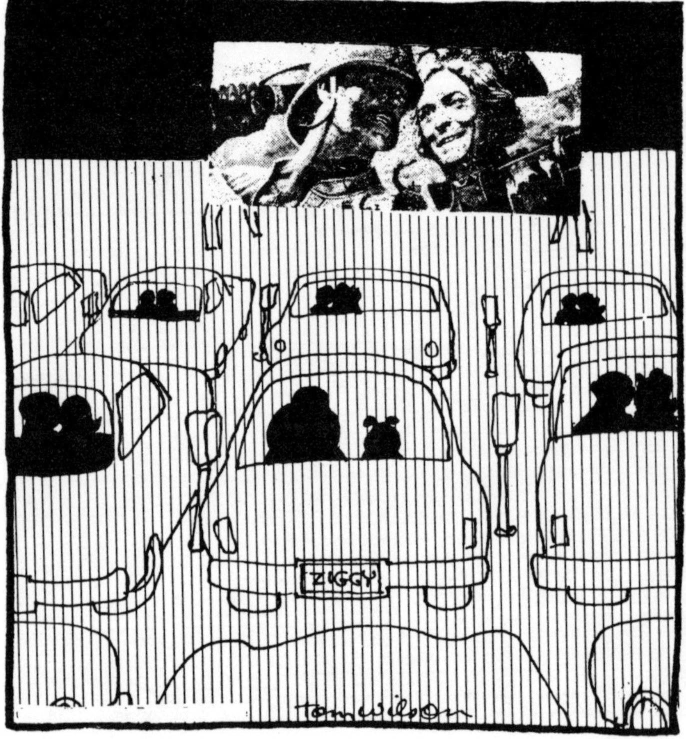
ZIGGY
tom wilson

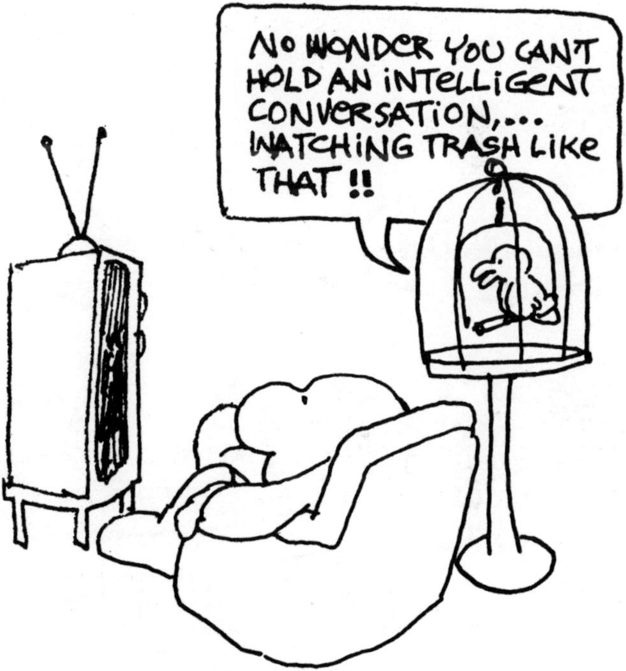
NO WONDER YOU CAN'T HOLD AN INTELLIGENT CONVERSATION,... WATCHING TRASH LIKE THAT !!

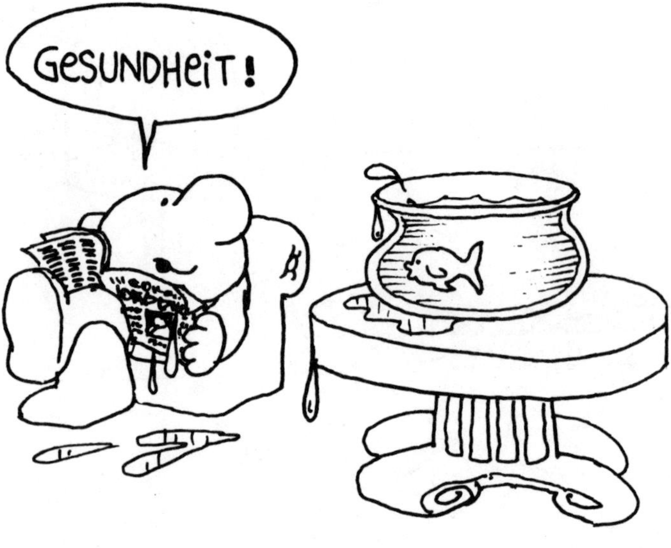
GESUNDHEIT!

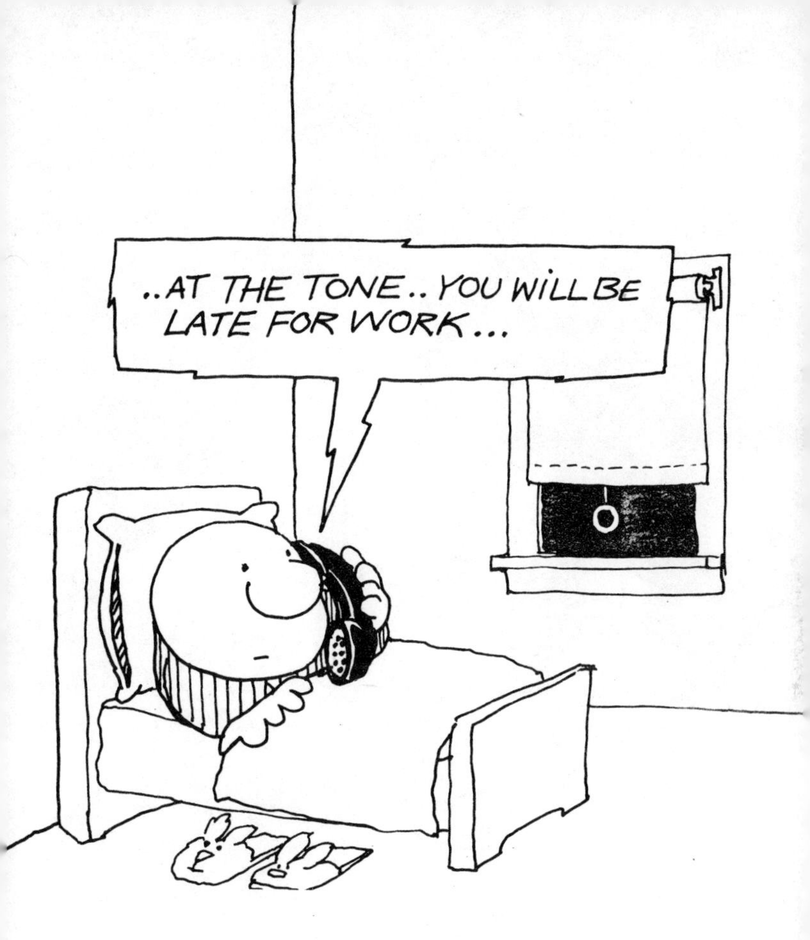
..AT THE TONE.. YOU WILL BE LATE FOR WORK...

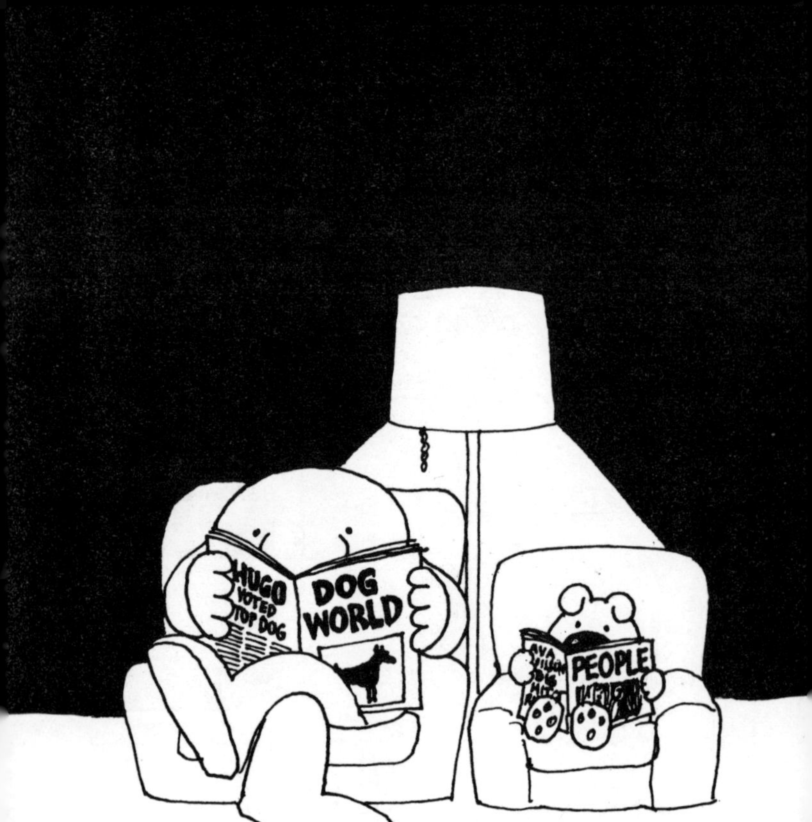
HUGO VOTED TOP DOG
DOG WORLD
PEOPLE

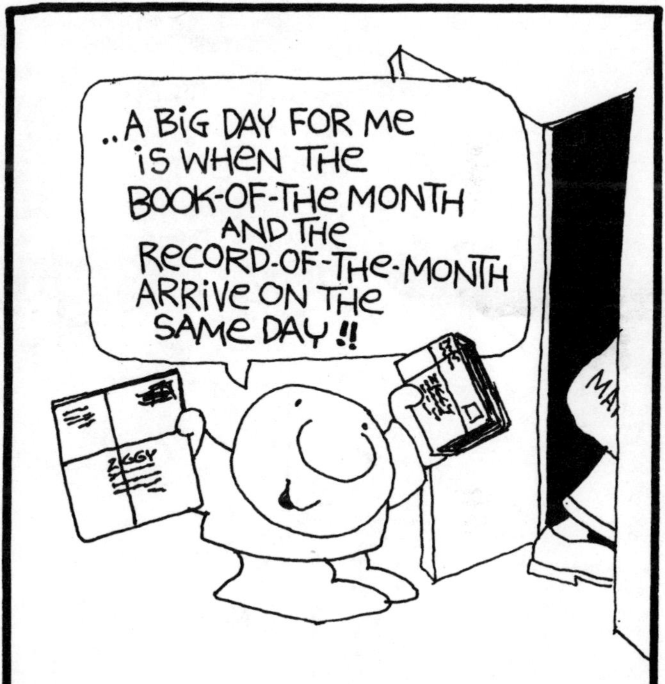
..A BIG DAY FOR ME IS WHEN THE BOOK-OF-THE MONTH AND THE RECORD-OF-THE-MONTH ARRIVE ON THE SAME DAY !!

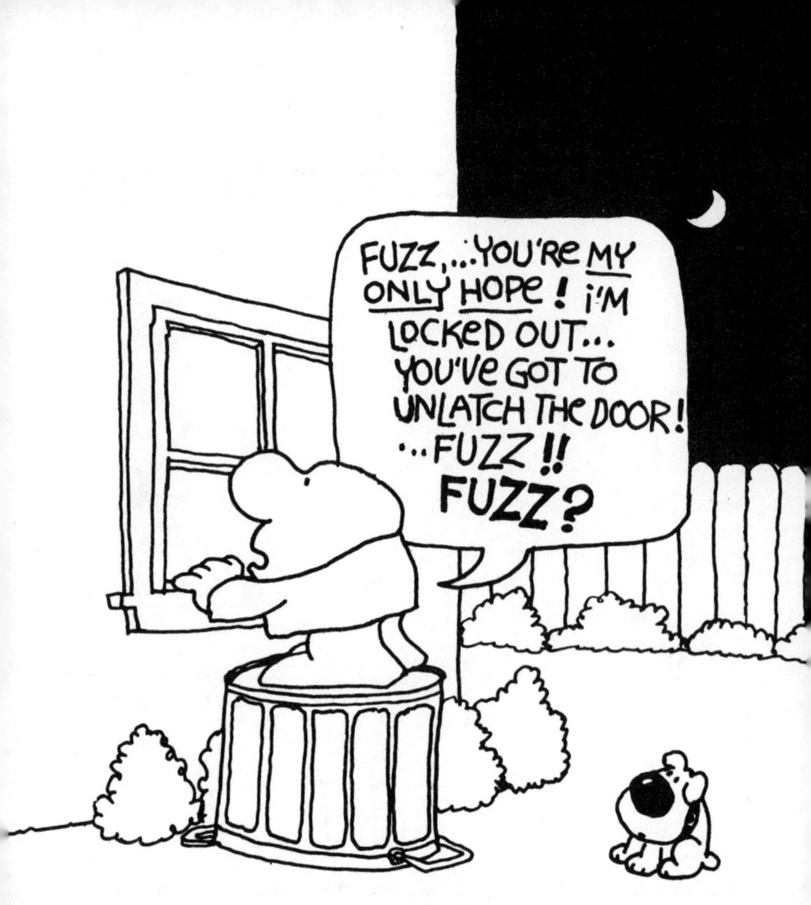
FUZZ,...YOU'RE MY ONLY HOPE! I'M LOCKED OUT... YOU'VE GOT TO UNLATCH THE DOOR! ...FUZZ!! FUZZ?

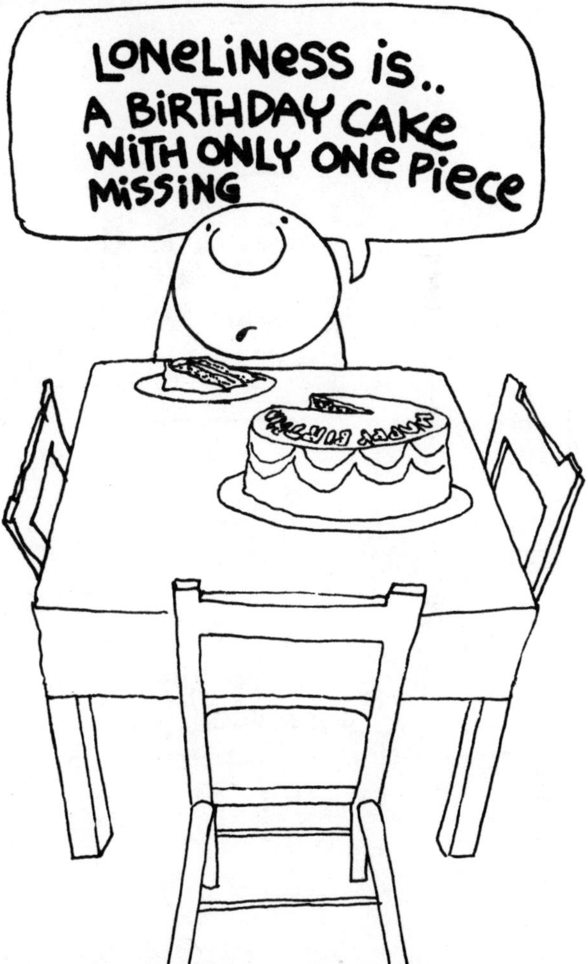
LONELINESS IS..
A BIRTHDAY CAKE
WITH ONLY ONE PIECE
MISSING

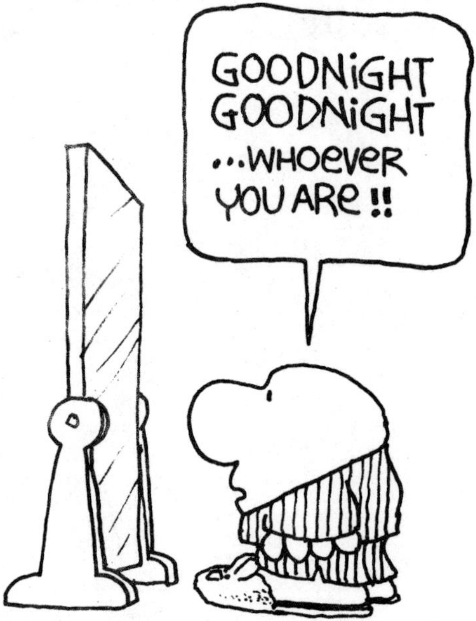
GOODNIGHT GOODNIGHT ...WHOEVER YOU ARE !!